Measuring Time

What is Time?

Tracey Steffora

KU-325-008

www.raintreepublishers.co.uk
Visit our website to find out more information about Raintree books.

To order:
☎ Phone 0845 6044371
▤ Fax +44 (0) 1865 312263
✉ Email myorders@raintreepublishers.co.uk

Customers from outside the UK please telephone +44 1865 312262

Raintree is an imprint of Capstone Global Library Limited, a company incorporated in England and Wales having its registered office at 7 Pilgrim Street, London, EC4V 6LB – Registered company number: 6695582

Text © Capstone Global Library Limited 2012
First published in hardback in 2012
First published in paperback in 2013
The moral rights of the proprietor have been asserted.

All rights reserved. No part of this publication may be reproduced in any form or by any means (including photocopying or storing it in any medium by electronic means and whether or not transiently or incidentally to some other use of this publication) without the written permission of the copyright owner, except in accordance with the provisions of the Copyright, Designs and Patents Act 1988 or under the terms of a licence issued by the Copyright Licensing Agency, Saffron House, 6–10 Kirby Street, London EC1N 8TS (www.cla.co.uk). Applications for the copyright owner's written permission should be addressed to the publisher.

Edited by Daniel Nunn, Rebecca Rissman, and Harriet Milles
Designed by Richard Parker
Picture research by Hannah Taylor
Illustrations © Capstone Global Library Ltd.
Originated by Capstone Global Library Ltd.
Production by Victoria Fitzgerald
Printed and bound in China by Leo Paper Products Ltd

ISBN 978 1 406 22903 5 (hardback)
15 14 13 12 11
10 9 8 7 6 5 4 3 2 1

ISBN 978 1 406 22967 7 (paperback)
16 15 14 13 12
10 9 8 7 6 5 4 3 2 1

British Library Cataloguing in Publication Data
Steffora, Tracey.
  What is time?. – (Acorn plus)
  1. Time–Pictorial works–Juvenile literature.
  I. Title II. Series
  529-dc22
A full catalogue record for this book is available from the British Library.

Acknowledgements
We would like to thank the following for permission to reproduce photographs: Alamy Images **pp. 4** (© Asia Images Group Pte Ltd), **5** (© Profimedia International s.r.o.), **9, 11** (© Greatstock Photographic Library), **21** (© STOCK4B GmbH); iStockphoto **pp. 13 left** (© Robert Kneschke), **17** (© tBoyan), **19** (© Dejan Ristovski), **20** (© Rob Broek); Photolibrary **p. 8** (Comstock); Shutterstock **pp. 6** (© kolosigor), **7** (© John Wollwerth), **10** (© wavebreakmedia ltd), **12** (© Paul Aniszewski), **13 middle** (© Monkey Business Images), **13 right** (© Benjamin Haas), **15** (© R-photos).

Cover photograph of traditional alarm clocks reproduced with permission of Shutterstock (© Mike Flippo).

We would like to thank Patricia Wooster for her invaluable help in the preparation of this book.

Every effort has been made to contact copyright holders of any material reproduced in this book. Any omissions will be rectified in subsequent printings if notice is given to the publisher.

MORAY COUNCIL
LIBRARIES &
INFO.SERVICES

20 34 90 22

Askews & Holts

J529

Contents

Some words appear in bold, **like this**. You can find out what they mean in "Words to know" on page 23.

What is time?

Have you ever had to wait for something to happen? **Measuring** time helps us know when things are going to happen.

Do you ever wonder how long something takes?

We use time to measure how long something takes.

Time is a way we order **events**.

Seconds

Some things take a short amount of time. A **second** is a very short amount of time. It takes about a second to blow out a candle.

You use seconds to **measure** how long you can hold your breath.

Minutes

minute timer

A **minute** is longer than a **second**. There are 60 seconds in one minute.

You use minutes to **measure** how long it takes to walk somewhere.

Hours

one hour

An **hour** is longer than a **minute**. There are 60 minutes in one hour.

You use hours to **measure** how long you are at school each **day**.

Days

A **day** is longer than an **hour**. There are 24 hours in one day.

morning

afternoon

night

Every day has a morning, **afternoon**, and night.

Weeks

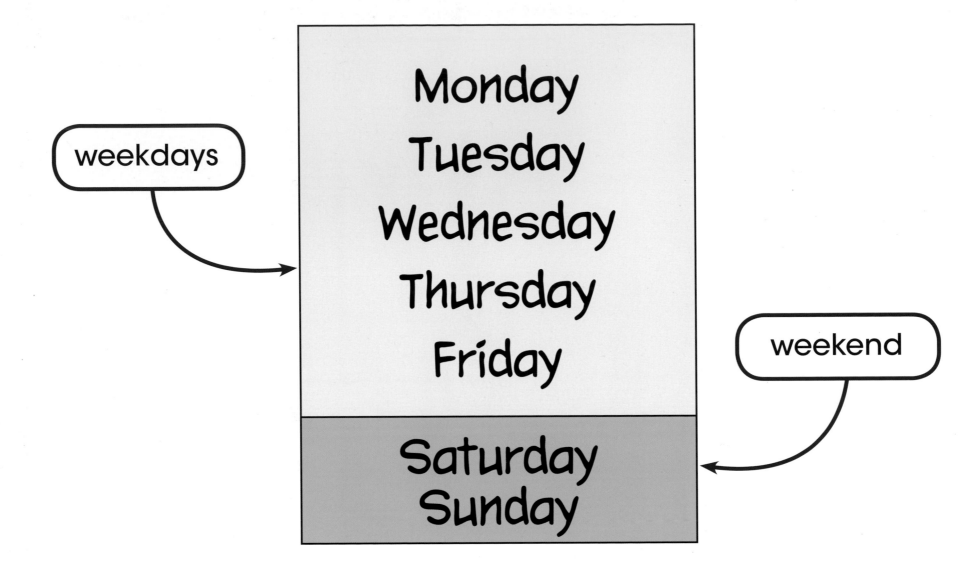

A **week** is longer than a **day**. There are seven days in one week.

You use weeks to **measure** how long it takes for a plant to grow.

Months and seasons

April						
Sunday	Monday	Tuesday	Wednesday	Thursday	Friday	Saturday
					1	2
3	4	5	6	7	8	9
10	11	12	13	14	15	16
17	18	19	20	21	22	23
24	25	26	27	28	29	30

one week

A **month** is longer than a **week**. There are just over four full weeks in one month.

spring

summer

autumn

winter

You use months to **measure seasons**. There are four seasons in one **year**. The seasons are called spring, summer, autumn, and winter.

Years

one month

JANUARY

Sunday	Monday	Tuesday	Wednesday	Thursday	Friday	Saturday
						1
2	3	4	5	6	7	8
9	10	11	12	13	14	15
16	17	18	19	20	21	22
23	24	25	26	27	28	29
30	31					

FEBRUARY

Sunday	Monday	Tuesday	Wednesday	Thursday	Friday	Saturday
		1	2	3	4	5
6	7	8	9	10	11	12
13	14	15	16	17	18	19
20	21	22	23	24	25	26
27	28					

MARCH

Sunday	Monday	Tuesday	Wednesday	Thursday	Friday	Saturday
		1	2	3	4	5
6	7	8	9	10	11	12
13	14	15	16	17	18	19
20	21	22	23	24	25	26
27	28	29	30	31		

APRIL

Sunday	Monday	Tuesday	Wednesday	Thursday	Friday	Saturday
					1	2
3	4	5	6	7	8	9
10	11	12	13	14	15	16
17	18	19	20	21	22	23
24	25	26	27	28	29	30

MAY

Sunday	Monday	Tuesday	Wednesday	Thursday	Friday	Saturday
1	2	3	4	5	6	7
8	9	10	11	12	13	14
15	16	17	18	19	20	21
22	23	24	25	26	27	28
29	30	31				

JUNE

Sunday	Monday	Tuesday	Wednesday	Thursday	Friday	Saturday
			1	2	3	4
5	6	7	8	9	10	11
12	13	14	15	16	17	18
19	20	21	22	23	24	25
26	27	28	29	30		

JULY

Sunday	Monday	Tuesday	Wednesday	Thursday	Friday	Saturday
					1	2
3	4	5	6	7	8	9
10	11	12	13	14	15	16
17	18	19	20	21	22	23
24	25	26	27	28	29	30
31						

AUGUST

Sunday	Monday	Tuesday	Wednesday	Thursday	Friday	Saturday
	1	2	3	4	5	6
7	8	9	10	11	12	13
14	15	16	17	18	19	20
21	22	23	24	25	26	27
28	29	30	31			

SEPTEMBER

Sunday	Monday	Tuesday	Wednesday	Thursday	Friday	Saturday
				1	2	3
4	5	6	7	8	9	10
11	12	13	14	15	16	17
18	19	20	21	22	23	24
25	26	27	28	29	30	

OCTOBER

Sunday	Monday	Tuesday	Wednesday	Thursday	Friday	Saturday
						1
2	3	4	5	6	7	8
9	10	11	12	13	14	15
16	17	18	19	20	21	22
23	24	25	26	27	28	29
30	31					

NOVEMBER

Sunday	Monday	Tuesday	Wednesday	Thursday	Friday	Saturday
		1	2	3	4	5
6	7	8	9	10	11	12
13	14	15	16	17	18	19
20	21	22	23	24	25	26
27	28	29	30			

DECEMBER

Sunday	Monday	Tuesday	Wednesday	Thursday	Friday	Saturday
				1	2	3
4	5	6	7	8	9	10
11	12	13	14	15	16	17
18	19	20	21	22	23	24
25	26	27	28	29	30	31

A **year** is a long amount of time. There are twelve **months** in one year. There are 365 **days** in one year.

You use years to **measure** how old you are.

Telling time

clock

There are special tools that help us **measure** and tell the time. **Clocks** measure shorter amounts of time. Clocks measure **seconds**, **minutes**, and **hours**.

calendar

Calendars measure longer amounts of time.
Calendars measure **days**, **weeks**, **months**, and **years**.

Time vocabulary

Monday   Tuesday   Wednesday   Thursday   Friday   Saturday   Sunday

We use special words that help us know when things will happen. Some of these words are:

yesterday	first	before
today	next	after
tomorrow	last	soon

Monday is the *first* **day** of the **week**.

The *next* day is Tuesday.

Tuesday is *after* Monday.

If *today* is Monday, *tomorrow* will be Tuesday.

Words to know

afternoon time of the day that comes after the morning

calendar list of the days, weeks, and months of a year

clock tool that tells you what time it is

day period of 24 hours. Each day has a morning, an afternoon, and night time.

event thing that happens or is going to happen

hour 60 minutes of time

measure to learn the size, amount, or speed of something

minute 60 seconds of time

month just over four full weeks of time

seasons four main periods of time that make up a year. The seasons are spring, summer, autumn, and winter.

second a very short amount of time

week seven days of time. The days in a week are called Monday, Tuesday, Wednesday, Thursday, Friday, Saturday, and Sunday.

year 12 months of time

Index

Notes for parents and teachers

Before reading

Show the children the front cover of the book. Guide children in a discussion about what they know about time. Explain to children that measuring time helps us know when things are going to happen.

After reading

- Gather the children into a group. Ask them to think of some common activities. Possible activities can be: walking across the classroom, reading one page in a book to a partner, washing their hands, or reading a poem. Write down their suggestions on the board. Then, using a stopwatch, time different volunteers as they do each activity. Record the times on the board.